If You Were Me and Lived In...
CUBA

A Child's Introduction to Culture Around the World

Carole P. Roman
Illustrated by Kelsea Wierenga

For Kelsea. Thanks for everything.

Special thanks to Rudy Acosta for the all the information and a great meal.

Copyright © 2017 Carole P. Roman

All rights reserved.

ISBN: 1-947118-88-9

ISBN 13: 978-1-947118-88-1

Disclaimer:

Please note that there may be differences in dialect that will vary according to region. Multiple individuals (from each country) were used as sources for the pronunciation key but you should be aware of the possibility of alternative pronunciations.

If you were me and lived in Cuba (Cue-ba), you would live on an island located in the northern Caribbean (Ka-rih-bee-an) in the western hemisphere. It is known as the Republic of Cuba and is the biggest island in the Caribbean and the second most populated in the area. You would live in the capital and largest city, Havana (Huh-van-uh). You would love the energy of this busy port. It is an important business and banking center for the whole island.

Havana is located on a bay and has three major harbors. A bay is a small half-circle of water that has ocean on one side and land on the other. The Almendares (Al-men-dar-res) River crosses through the city, separating it from north to south.

Havana is an old city. It was founded by Spanish explorers in the 16th century and served as a vital harbor for the treasure-filled ships traveling from the New World back to Spain.

Your parents might have picked the name Veronica (Ver-on-ik-ah), Zamira (Za-mir-ah), or Aymee (Aye-maye) if you were a girl. Ernesto (Ur-nest-oh), José (Hoe-say), and Luis (Loo-ees) were their choices if you were a boy.

When you get home from school, Mami (Ma-me) is waiting for you. Papi (Pa-pee) comes much later when he finishes working at his office. Can you guess who we are talking about?

Abuela (Ah-bew-la) is what you call your grandmother. She comes on Saturday to watch you for a few hours. She brings lots of Cuban Convertible Pesos (Cue-ban Kun-ver-tuh-buhl Pey-sos) when you go shopping together.

Mami made a list. You need huevos (wey-vohs), queso (kay-so), and pan (paen) to make a bocadillo (bo-cah-dee-yo). If a bocodillo is a sandwich, can you guess what fillings your abelua has purchased?

Abuela says don't forget the leche (le-chey); she wants to make cafe con leche (ka-fay con le-chey). You hope she gives you a sip. She says, "Be careful! Muy caliente.(moo-ee cal-ee-yen-tay)."

When visitors come to Cuba, you make sure you take them to see the Castillo del Morro (Kahs-tee-yoh del Mor-o). It is an old Spanish fort built in the 17th century.

Construction for the castle started in 1587 but took many years to finish it. The Castillo del Morro was built to protect Cuba from pirates, but it was also used as a prison. You like to run up and down the stairs of the many levels and pretend you were living in the olden days.

At nine o'clock every night, there is a special event reminding people the important role the castle played in Cuba's history. Actors dress up as soldiers in uniforms from three hundred years ago. They create a show that includes a ceremony called Cañonazo de las Nueves (Can-yo-nas-zo de las Nu-ey-vez) which literally means shooting the cannons at nine. The evening ends with a loud bang that can be heard far away!

Mami prefers to go to Cayo Coco (Ca-yo Co-co), which is a beautiful beach. It is part of an archipelago (ar-kuh-pel-uh-go), which means it is in a chain of islands and can only be reached by airplane or by a bridge. It is said that the famous author Ernest Hemingway used this beach as a background for his novels.

Mami always makes your favorite dishes for your cumpleaños (kum-pley-an-os). Your birthday is a special day for celebration and good food. You would start the meal with tostones (toas-ton-es). You love the crispy twice-fried plantains (plan-tains). Some people think they look like bananas. They are in the banana family but can't be eaten raw. You helped make the garlic and sour orange mojo (moh-hoh) sauce to dip the starchy fruit. Next comes arroz con pollo (ah-raws kon pol-yo), which is chicken and rice. You can't wait for ropa vieja (rope-ah vee-aye-ha) to be put on the table. The shredded beef with colorful vegetables is a family favorite.

If there is a lot of company, Papi will roast a whole pig. Moros y Cristianos (Mor-os ey Cris-tee-an-os) is the name for black beans and rice. You eat it every night. You remind them not to forget the papas rellenas (pa-pas rel-len-as), because you love stuffed potatoes.

Of course, you finish the meal with tres leches (trace lech-es) cake. You would say "Buen provecho" (Bwen pro-veh-cho), which means enjoy the meal.

Baseball is an important game in Cuba. Whether you are watching a game with Papi or playing with your friends, you love this ball game.

Papi always says that Cuba competes extremely well in international sporting events, particularly in boxing and athletics. He said that is because of the government's encouragement and support in this field, as it sees sports as a necessary part of education. In 1991, Cuba hosted the Pan-American Games, the most important sporting event held in the country.

When you watch the Olympic Games, everyone is proudest of the boxers, who usually win the largest number of medals. Almost every town has gyms that host frequent boxing tournaments.

You were taught that sports are an essential part of life and being good can only come from hard work and practice. Your parents began exercising with you when you were only forty-five days old!

Mami exercised and massaged your arms and legs when you were young to make you strong. You played lots of games and didn't even know you were exercising!

July 18th to the 27th is a special time in Cuba. It is when the carnival at Santiago de Cuba (San-tee-ah-go de Cue-ba) is held. It is a weeklong festival that celebrates Cuban traditions dating back hundreds of years. There is a lot of dancing, singing, music, and costumes. It combines all the different cultures and traditions of the diverse people who make up the population of Cuba and can include, African, Natives, Spanish, and French.

You love the first day because it is the biggest celebration.

You stay in a hotel, and if you are lucky, you arrive in early July to see the annual Fire Festival, also known as Fiesta del Fuego (Fe-es-ta del Fuh-way-go).

You would tell all your friends about it when you go to la escuela (es-kwe-la). Can you guess where that is?

So you see, if you were me, how life in Cuba could really be.

Glossary

Abuela (Ah-bwe-la)- grandmother.

Almendares (Al-men-dar-res)- a river that crosses through the city, separating north to south.

archipelago (ar-kuh-pel-uh-go)- a chain of islands and can only be reached by airplane or by a bridge.

arroz con pollo (ah-raws kon pol-yo)- chicken and rice.

athletics (ath-led-iks)- sports such as running, boxing, etc.

Aymee (Aye-maye)- a popular girl's name in Cuba.

baseball (bas-ball)- a ball game played between two teams consisting of nine players on each team on a field in the shape of a diamond with four bases.

bay (bay)- a small half circle of water that has ocean on one side and land on the other.

bocadillo (bo-ca-dee-oh)- a Spanish term used for a ham, cheese, and tomato sandwich.

boxing (bok-sing)- a sport played by two people using their fists while wearing padded gloves in a roped-off square ring.

Buen provecho (Bwen pro-veh-cho)- "Enjoy the meal" in Spanish.

cafe con leche (kafay con lechay)- "coffee with milk" in Spanish.

Cañonazo de las Nuevas (Can-yo-nas-zo de las Nu-ey-vez)- shooting the cannons at nine.

Caribbean (Ka-rih-bee-an)- relating to the Caribbean island, sea, culture, food, or language.

carnival at Santiago de Cuba (karn-e-veil at San-tee-ah-go de Cue-ba)- held every July

18th to 27th. It is a weeklong festival that celebrates Cuban traditions.

Castillo del Morro (Kahs-tee-yoh del Mor-o)- an old Spanish fort built in the 17th century. It is located high on a hill looking over the Bay of Santiago.

(Ca-yo Co-co)- a popular and beautiful beach.

Cuba (Cue-ba)- a self-governed Caribbean Island.

Cuban Convertible Pesos (Cue-ban Kun-ver-tuh-buhl Pey-sos)- Cuba's currency.

cumpleaños (kum-pley-an-os)- birthday.

Ernest Hemingway (Ur-nest Hem-ing-way)- a 20th century famous author who used the Cayo Coco (Ca-yo Co-co) beach as a background for his novels.

Ernesto (Ur-nest-oh)- a popular boy's name in Cuba.

escuela (es-kwe-la)- a school.

exercise (ex-er-size)- activity that is for the purpose of conditioning the body to improve health.

Fiesta del Fuego (Fe-es-ta del Fuh-way-go)- the annual Fire Festival held early July.

Havana (Huh-van-uh)- the capital and largest city in Cuba.

huevos (wey-vohs)- eggs.

jamón (ham-un)- ham.

José (Hoe-say)- a popular boy's name in Cuba.

leche (le-chey)- milk.

Luis (Loo-ees)- a popular boy's name in Cuba.

Mami (Ma-me)- Mommy.

massage (ma-sahje)- rubbing and kneading the body's muscles and joints to relieve tension.

mojo (moh-joh)- a tart Cuban sauce for dipping, which usually consists of olive oil, minced garlic, lime juice, ground cumin, salt and pepper.

Moros y Cristianos (Mor-os ey Cris-tee-an-os)- a popular Cuban dish of rice and black beans.

muy caliente (moo-ee cal-ie-en-tay)- very hot.

pan (paen)- bread.

Pan-American Games (Pan-Amer-ay-can Games)- In 1991, Cuba hosted the Pan-American Games, the most prestigious sporting event held in the country.

papas rellenas (pa-pas rel-len-as)- dough made from baked potato filled with beef, chopped onions, olives, hard boiled eggs, and other spices and deep fried.

Papi (Pa-pee)- Daddy.

pirate (py-ret)- a thief who robs ships at sea in search for gold and other possessions.

plantains (plan-tains)- a plant that grows a fruit similar to bananas.

prison (priz-en)- a place of confinement to those who have broken the law.

queso (kay-so)- cheese.

Republic of Cuba (Re-pub-lic of Cue-ba)- the largest island in the Caribbean with the second largest population in the area.

ropa vieja (rope-ah vee-aye-ha)- shredded beef cooked with vegetables.

Santiago de Cuba (San-tee-ah-go de Cue-ba)- the second largest city in Cuba. Every July 18th to 27th a large event known as Carnival is held there. It is a weeklong festival that celebrates Cuban traditions.

tostones (toas-ton-es)- crispy twice-fried plantains.

tournament (torn-a-ment)- a set of games or challenges that compile into a competition.

tres leches (trace lech-es)- a popular cake served at events.

Veronica (Ver-on-ik-ah)- a popular girl's name in Cuba.

vital (vi-tal)- important and necessary.

Zamira (Za-mir-ah)- popular girl's name in Cuba.

www.ingramcontent.com/pod-product-compliance
Lightning Source LLC
Chambersburg PA
CBHW041501220426
43661CB00016B/1214